LOVE NEVER FAILS

A JOURNAL TO BE INSPIRED BY THE POWER OF LOVE

HILDA ST. CLAIR

PARACLETE PRESS
BREWSTER, MASSACHUSETTS

2017 First printing

Love Never Fails: A Journal to be Inspired by the Power of Love

Copyright © 2017 by The Community of Jesus, Inc.

ISBN 978-1-61261-832-6

Published by Paraclete Press
Brewster, Massachusetts
www.paracletepress.com

Printed in the United States of America

Introduction

Love—is there any other quality of human life that we want more of but know less about?

These pages hold some thoughtful insights into this great mystery from some of the world's most thought-ful people, from Sophocles to the Dalai Lama, from Ben Franklin to Maya Angelou. Some may make you wonder; some may touch your heart; some may even inspire you to do something. Read them, enjoy them, ponder them, remember them . . . live them. Gathered together as they are, they describe a love that never fails.

THREE THINGS WILL LAST
FOREVER—FAITH, HOPE, AND
LOVE—AND THE GREATEST
OF THESE IS LOVE.

1 CORINTHIANS 13:13

DRAW A CIRCLE WITH THE WORD "love" IN THE MIDDLE. NOW, WHERE WOULD YOU PLACE "FAITH" AND "HOPE"? Why?

OUR LIFE

IS ALL FOUNDED AND ROOTED
IN LOVE, AND WITHOUT LOVE
WE CANNOT LIVE.

JULIAN OF NORWICH

Make a *simple drawing* OF your LIFE as a Garden. IF LOVE were a PLANT IN THE Garden, WHAT KIND OF PLANT WOULD IT Be?

Name 3 ingredients you would need TO *"fertilize"* THIS PLANT.

I LOVE BECAUSE I LOVE;
I LOVE IN ORDER THAT I
MAY LOVE.

BERNARD OF CLAIRVAUX

WHO DO YOU KNOW LIKE THIS—
SOMEONE WHO
GIVES OUT LOVE
generously,
NO MATTER WHAT IS HAPPENING?

Write 2 sentences about that person.

Only
love

GIVES US
THE TASTE OF
ETERNITY.

JEWISH PROVERB

Imagine THAT YOU ARE ON A LONG, PEACEFUL BEACH WITH A PERFECT VIEW OF THE OCEAN.

LOOK AT THE *waves* AND THINK ABOUT SOMEONE YOU LOVE. NOW THINK ABOUT SOMEONE WHO LOVES YOU.

CLOSE YOUR EYES AND *enjoy* THIS SCENE.

I Have
DeciDeD TO
STICK WITH
LOVe....
HaTe is TOO
GreaT a
BurDeN TO
Bear.

Martin Luther King Jr.

WHAT MAKES HATRED SO HEAVY?

IF THE PILE OF ROCKS BELOW IS HATRED, NAME EACH ROCK THAT GOES INTO MAKING THE PILE SO HEAVY.

LOVE AND COMPASSION ARE
NECESSITIES, NOT LUXURIES.
WITHOUT THEM HUMANITY
CANNOT SURVIVE.

DALAI LAMA

Imagine that love is like **water**.

what can a cup of water do?

a water sprinkler?

a lake?

BEING DEEPLY
LOVED BY
SOMEONE
GIVES YOU
STRENGTH,
WHILE LOVING
SOMEONE
DEEPLY
GIVES YOU
COURAGE.

LAO TZU

What
would it
mean
for you
to be

courageous?

THINK OF A PLACE IN YOUR LIFE WHERE
you are afraid.
How would love
help you?

WHEN I DESPAIR, I REMEMBER
THAT ALL THROUGH HISTORY
THE WAY OF TRUTH AND LOVE
HAVE ALWAYS WON.

MAHATMA GANDHI

WRITE THE YEAR YOU WERE BORN.
WHAT WAS HAPPENING THEN?

WERE THERE ANY ACTS OF
HEROISM?

MAKE A SKETCH OF SOMETHING
good FROM THAT TIME.

I BELIEVE
THAT THE
WORLD
WAS
CREATED AND APPROVED BY
LOVE ... AND THAT ... IT CAN
BE REDEEMED ONLY BY LOVE.

WENDELL BERRY

IF YOU COULD DO *anything*
TO HELP THE
whole world,
ANYTHING AT ALL, WHAT WOULD IT BE?

IN THE SMALL BOX, WRITE AN **action** YOU
COULD TAKE RIGHT NOW.

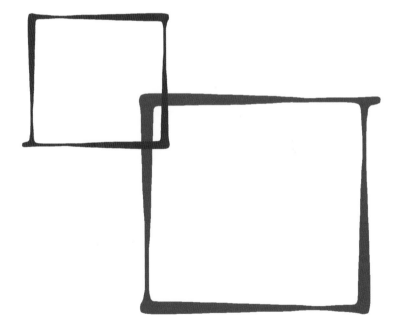

IN THE LARGE BOX, WRITE A **big dream** OF
SOMETHING YOU COULD DO.

One word FREES US OF ALL THE WEIGHT AND PAIN OF LIFE: THAT WORD IS LOVE.

SOPHOCLES

FIND SOME CRAYONS OR COLORED PENCILS.

COLOR IN THESE LETTERS AND THINK ABOUT
THE MANY WAYS LOVE FILLS YOUR LIFE.

LOVE

Why did you choose the
colors you used?

beauty

DUTY MAKES US
DO THINGS WELL,
BUT LOVE MAKES
US DO THEM
BEAUTIFULLY.

PHILLIPS BROOKS

MAKE A LIST of five "duties" in your life.

1. _____

2. _____

3. _____

4. _____

5. _____

Now, imagine each one fully motivated by love.

Would the list look any different? How?

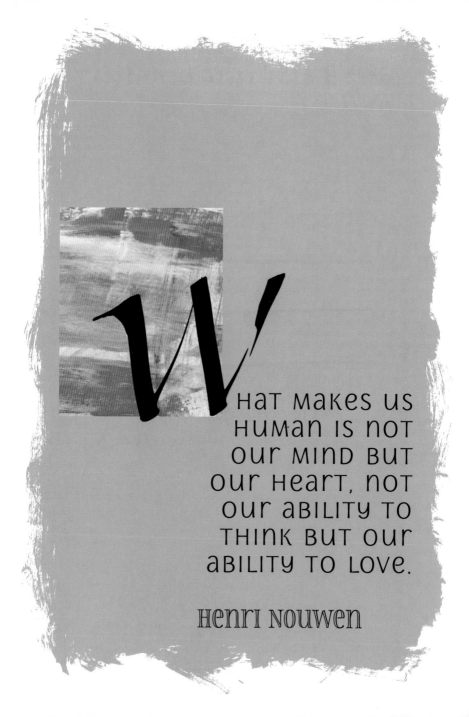

What makes us human is not our mind but our heart, not our ability to think but our ability to love.

HENRI NOUWEN

Did you have a ROLE MODEL when you were a child?

WHO WAS IT?

What did LOVE have to do with this person's influence on you?

Love

IS PATIENT AND KIND.

1 CORINTHIANS 13:4

LOVE

PATIENCE

KINDNESS

Draw a symbol for each of these words—a symbol that means something to you *personally*.

spread

LOVE

everywhere you go.
Let no one ever
come to you
without leaving happier.

MOTHER TERESA

PEOPLE
WHO COULD
USE MY HELP
TODAY

_____
_____
_____
_____
_____

_____
_____
_____
_____
_____

PEOPLE
I COULD
CALL

PEOPLE
I COULD
WRITE OR
EMAIL

_____
_____
_____
_____
_____

What does love look like?

IT HAS THE HANDS
TO HELP OTHERS.

AUGUSTINE OF HIPPO

In the ten fingers of these hands write times when someone HELPED you.

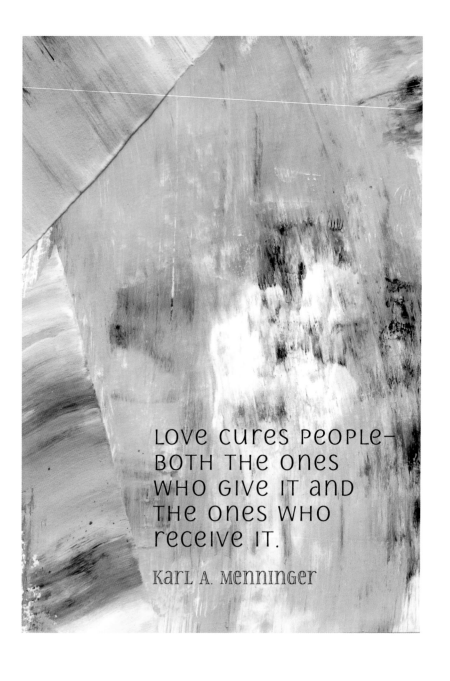

LOVE CURES PEOPLE—
BOTH THE ONES
WHO GIVE IT AND
THE ONES WHO
RECEIVE IT.

KARL A. MENNINGER

NAME A PERSON WHO HAS SHOWN

love

TO YOU. HOW HAVE YOU SHOWN LOVE BACK?

WHO ELSE COULD YOU SHOW LOVE TO?

the opposite

OF LOVE IS NOT HATE,
IT'S INDIFFERENCE.

ELIE WIESEL

On the left, write the names of four people you'd like to have a better connection with. On the right, write one thing it would take for you to make that connection with them.

TO LOVE AT ALL IS
TO BE VULNERABLE.
LOVE ANYTHING
AND YOUR HEART
WILL BE
WRUNG
AND POSSIBLY
BROKEN.

C. S. Lewis.

Do you have a broken heart?
Has your heart ever been broken? If so, you
risked something.

Color in this award for yourself and add
words like...

I have loved!

I am a lover!

or even,

I survived!

IT TAKES COURAGE TO LOVE,
BUT PAIN THROUGH LOVE IS THE
PURIFYING FIRE WHICH THOSE
WHO LOVE GENEROUSLY KNOW.

Eleanor Roosevelt

IN THESE FLAMES

WRITE ABOUT A
TIME YOU WERE
IN PAIN BECAUSE
OF LOVING
SOMEONE.

What good came out of the experience?

WHEN WE
LOVE,
WE ALWAYS
STRIVE TO BECOME BETTER
THAN WE ARE.

PAULO COELHO

Who is a hero for you?

Name three qualities that make that person a hero.

1.

2.

3.

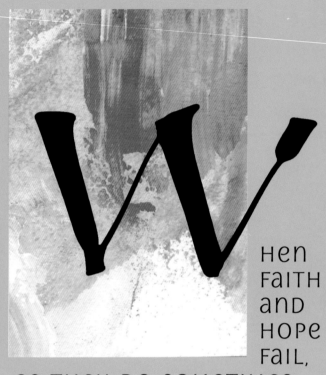

When
Faith
and
Hope
Fail,
as they do sometimes,
we must try charity,
which is love in action.

DINAH MARIA CRAIK

IF YOU WERE AT A HOTEL CALLED *The Last Resort*, A PLACE WHERE LOVE CHANGES THINGS, WHO or WHAT WOULD YOU WANT WITH YOU?

I BELIEVE
THAT LIFE
IS GIVEN US SO THAT WE
MAY GROW IN LOVE.

HELEN KELLER

THINK OF SOMEONE IN YOUR LIFE
WHO IS PARTICULARLY DIFFICULT TO LOVE. WHAT WOULD
YOU HAVE TO DO TO

grow in love

FOR THIS PERSON?

Love

IS NOT ... PROUD.

1 CORINTHIANS 13:4

Name two relationships

or situations in your life
where you need to be

More Humble.

what are ways you can practice humility
in those relationships or situations?

IF YOU WOULD
BE LOVED,
LOVE, AND BE
LOVABLE.

WHAT IS A *loving* PERSON?

_____

_____

WHAT IS A *lovable* PERSON?

_____

_____

HOW COULD YOU EXPRESS *more love?*

_____

_____

Lord

GRANT THAT I MIGHT
NOT SO MUCH SEEK TO
BE LOVED AS TO LOVE.

FRANCIS OF ASSISI

What keeps you from becoming more loving?

ON SOME OF THESE BRICKS WRITE THE THINGS
THAT KEEP YOU FROM BEING MORE LOVING.
ON THE HAMMER, WRITE WHAT LOVE WOULD DO TO
BREAK DOWN THAT WALL.

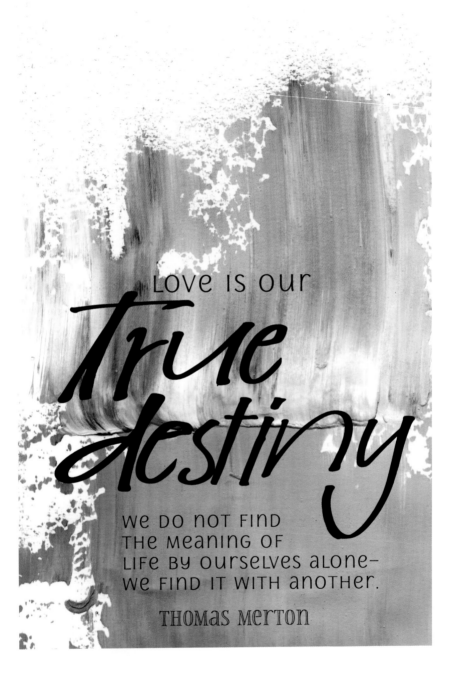

LOVE IS OUR

True

destiny

WE DO NOT FIND
THE MEANING OF
LIFE BY OURSELVES ALONE—
WE FIND IT WITH ANOTHER.

THOMAS MERTON

IN THE CIRCLE, WRITE THE NAMES
OF AT LEAST THREE PEOPLE
WHO ARE TEACHING YOU

the meaning of love.

NEXT TO EACH NAME WRITE ONE WAY YOU CAN
THANK THAT PERSON.

perHaps everytHinG
tHat friGHtens us
is, in its deepest
essence, sometHinG
HeLpLess tHat wants
our Love.

Rainer Maria Rilke

Who scares you? Why?

IN THE DRAWING PUT THE
INITIALS OF ONE WHO SCARES YOU, AND YOUR
OWN INITIALS IN THE OTHER PERSON.
NOW, COLOR THE WAVES BETWEEN YOU.

How can you show love to that person?

The greatest happiness of life
is the conviction that we are loved;
loved for ourselves, or rather
in spite of ourselves.

Victor Hugo

LIGHT a candle or draw a lit candle below. Spend at least three minutes thinking about the people who love you.

Now, spend at least three minutes thinking about how you can show them love in return.

Dare to love
and to be a
real friend.

Henri Nouwen

HAS A GOOD THING HAPPENED TO A FRIEND?
WHAT CAN YOU DO TO CELEBRATE IT TOGETHER?
Make plans below.

[I]F WE ARE BOLD,
LOVE STRIKES AWAY
THE CHAINS OF
FEAR FROM OUR
SOULS.

Maya Angelou

TAKE A WALK OUTDOORS, or
look through a magazine,
AND LOOK FOR SOMETHING THAT REMINDS
YOU OF BOLDNESS AND LOVE.

WHERE CAN
YOU LOVE
MORE
BOLDLY?

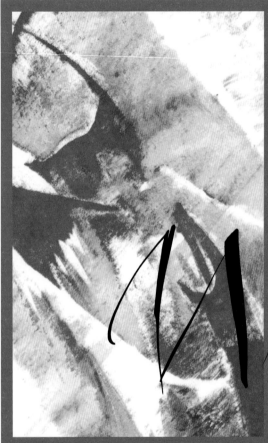

Here love exists, it works great things. But when it ceases to act, it ceases to exist.

GREGORY THE GREAT

WHAT ACT OF LOVE IS BEING REQUIRED OF YOU
TODAY?

AFTER YOU HAVE DONE IT,
check the box below
AND TAKE A MINUTE TO BE HAPPY
ABOUT THE STEP YOU TOOK.

THE *first duty*

OF LOVE IS TO LISTEN.

PAUL TILLICH

What does listening have to do with love? What three things do you need to do to become a better listener?

LOVE SEEKS ONE THING
ONLY: THE GOOD OF THE
ONE LOVED....
LOVE, THEREFORE,
IS ITS OWN REWARD.
          THOMAS MERTON

THINK ABOUT A TOUGH DECISION
YOU ONCE MADE.

WHAT MADE YOU DO IT?

WHAT ROLE DID LOVE PLAY?

Forgiveness is the final form of Love.

REINHOLD NIEBUHR

THINK OF SOMEONE WHO HAS HURT YOU.

TAKE YOUR HURT FEELINGS AND LET THEM GO.

MAKE A SIMPLE DRAWING IN THE SPACE BELOW, AND ENTITLE IT

"A New Day."

When you love someone,
you love the person
as they are, and
not as you'd like them
to be

Leo Tolstoy

ADD COLOR TO THE LETTERS BELOW.

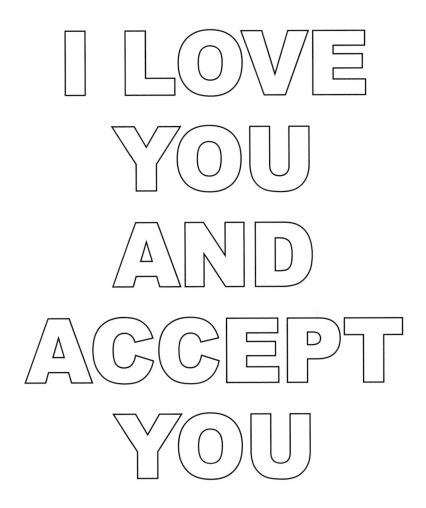

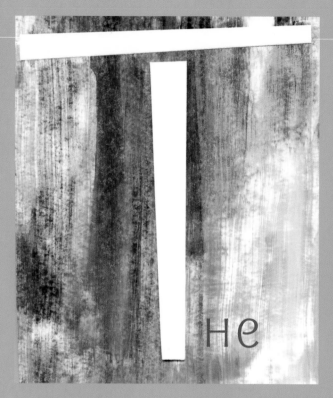

The

GROUND OF MERCY IS
LOVE, AND THE
WORKING OF MERCY
IS OUR KEEPING
IN LOVE

Julian of Norwich

Color in the flower below
with colors that speak to you
of mercy.

Who DO YOU NEED TO "GIVE"
THIS FLOWER TO TODAY?

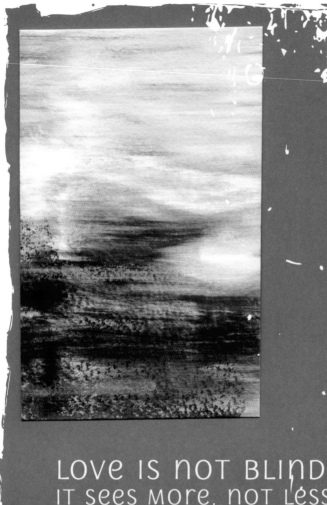

LOVE IS NOT BLIND—
IT SEES MORE, NOT LESS.
BUT BECAUSE IT SEES
MORE, IT IS WILLING TO
SEE LESS.
RABBI JULIUS GORDON

THINK OF SOMEONE WHO GETS ON
YOUR NERVES OR EVEN IRRITATES YOU.
LIST THREE REASONS WHY.

CAN YOU SEE THROUGH EACH OF THESE THREE
THINGS TO THE DEEPER PERSON WITHIN?

What do you see?

LOVE IS LIKE DEW
THAT FALLS ON BOTH
NETTLES AND LILIES.

Swedish Proverb

DO SOMETHING THOUGHTFUL FOR SOMEONE WITH
WHOM YOU DO NOT USUALLY ASSOCIATE.

DO IT WITHOUT LOOKING FOR ANY
recognition.

Draw an emoji (such as a smiley face) that shows
HOW YOU FEEL INSIDE AFTER DOING THIS.

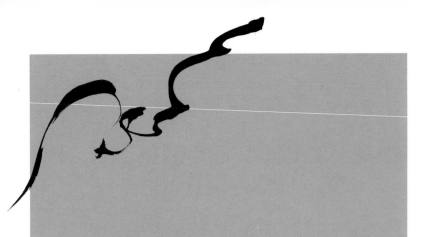

TO LOVE IS TO WILL THE GOOD OF THE OTHER.

THOMAS AQUINAS

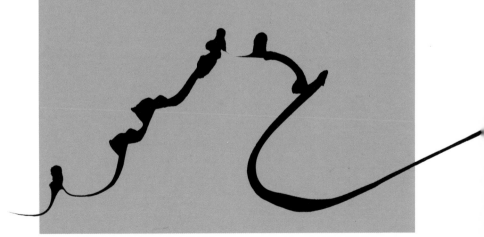

IMAGINE THE FIGURE BELOW IS SOMEONE WHO NEEDS TO KNOW LOVE, OR SOMEONE YOU ARE HAVING DIFFICULTY LOVING.

Write THREE *wonderful* THINGS YOU CAN IMAGINE HAPPENING FOR THAT PERSON.

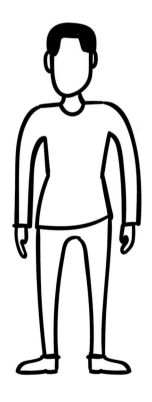

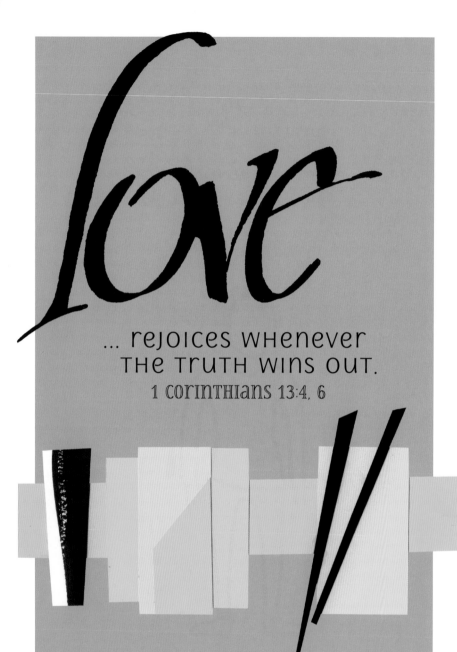

Love

... rejoices whenever the truth wins out.

1 Corinthians 13:4, 6

Are you in a disagreement with someone?

WHAT WOULD IT MEAN FOR THE "TRUTH" TO WIN THE ARGUMENT?

LOVE RECOGNIZES NO BARRIERS.
IT JUMPS HURDLES, LEAPS
FENCES, PENETRATES WALLS
TO ARRIVE AT ITS DESTINATION
FULL OF HOPE.
MAYA ANGELOU

WHO DO YOU IMAGINE ARE THE TWO FIGURES BELOW WHO ARE SEPARATED BY THE WALL/FENCE?

WHICH PERSON NEEDS TO MAKE THE
FIRST MOVE?

WHAT DOES HE/SHE NEED TO DO TO GET OVER THE WALL? HOW CAN YOU HELP IT TO HAPPEN?

The hunger for love
is much more difficult
to remove than the
hunger for bread.

MOTHER TERESA

NAME THREE THINGS YOU HUNGER FOR.
Write THESE THINGS IN THE SPACE BELOW.

UNDER EACH LINE WRITE A WORD OR A PHRASE THAT
SHOWS HOW LOVE CAN SATISFY EACH OF THESE
HUNGERS.

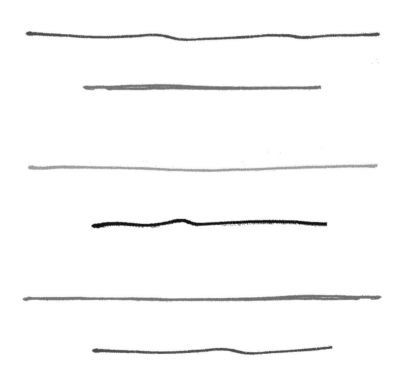

Love takes off masks
that we fear we
cannot live without
and know we
cannot live within.
James Baldwin

THINK OF SOMEONE WITH WHOM YOU NEED TO HAVE
an HONEST CONVERSATION.

Write WHEN YOU PLAN TO DO THIS AND
WHAT YOU'D REALLY LIKE TO TALK ABOUT.

A loving heart
is the
truest wisdom.

CHARLES DICKENS

WHAT WAS THE BEST PIECE OF ADVICE YOU ever received from a loved one? WHAT DID YOUR HEART HEAR?

Write THESE WORDS IN THE HEART BELOW.

MARTIN
LUTHER
KING,
JR.

Darkness cannot drive out
darkness: only light can do that.

Hate cannot drive out hate:
only love can do that.

LIGHT a CANDLE IN GRATITUDE

FOR THE HEROES IN YOUR LIFE.

Write ONE OF THEM A SINCERE LETTER OF THANKS IN THE SPACE BELOW.

An act of love, a voluntary taking on oneself of some of the pain of the world, increases the courage and love and hope of all.

DOROTHY DAY

Who in your life HAS SHARED YOUR WORRIES? HOW DID HE OR SHE LIGHTEN YOUR LOAD?

IN THE BACKPACK, WRITE YOUR PRESENT WORRIES.

THEN FIND A FRIEND TO SHARE THEM WITH. THEY WILL NO LONGER BE YOURS TO CARRY ALONE.

An
ounce
OF
LOVE
IS WORTH A POUND
OF KNOWLEDGE.

John Wesley

Have you ever given
KNOWLEDGE
when love would
have been a
better choice?

Imagine
if you had given
love instead.

What would that look like?

THE THINGS
THAT WE *love*

TELL US WHAT WE ARE.
THOMAS AQUINAS

CLOSE YOUR EYES. WHAT IS YOUR MOST VALUED POSSESSION? OF ALL THE OBJECTS YOU OWN, WHAT BRINGS YOU THE MOST *joy?*

DRAW THAT OBJECT HERE.

WHAT DOES THIS REFLECT ABOUT YOU?

Today, PEOPLE ARE
SUFFERING FROM POVERTY,
BUT ALSO FROM A LACK OF LOVE.

POPE FRANCIS

With markers or colored pencils, add color to this drawing of our world.

Pray for love to come into troubled areas.

Love

never gives up ...
is always hopeful, and
endures through every
circumstance.
1 Corinthians 13:7

LIST 3 PLACES IN YOUR LIFE
WHERE YOU NEED TO
HOPE.

1.

2.

3.

WHAT WOULD
ENDURANCE
BE FOR YOU TODAY?

WHERE THERE IS
LOVE, THERE IS NO
DARKNESS.

African Proverb

Think of the dark places in your life today. How many of them are inside of you?

LIGHT a
CANDLE OR
TURN ON A
LIGHT AND
PRAY FOR
LOVE TO
enter in.

ONLY *love* FILLS THE EMPTY SPACES CAUSED BY EVIL.

POPE FRANCIS

LET THE EMPTY HEART BELOW represent a person or place in *great need* TODAY.

FILL IN THE HEART WITH

ONE OR MORE COLORS AND LIST

WHAT EACH COLOR REPRESENTS

FOR MAKING THIS HEART

whole.

_____

_____

_____

_____

_____

AT THE EVENING OF LIFE, WE SHALL BE JUDGED ON OUR LOVE.

St. John of the Cross

Make a list of five people you love. how can you show love to each of them?

WHOSO LOVES, BELIEVES
THE IMPOSSIBLE.

ELIZABETH BARRETT BROWNING

WRITE THREE SEEMINGLY IMPOSSIBLE GOALS FOR SOMEONE OR ONES YOU LOVE.

WRITE NEXT TO EACH ONE, *I love you,* AND *I believe for you.*

I have found
the paradox,
that if you
love until it
hurts, there
can be no
more hurt,
only more
love.

MOTHER TERESA

IF YOU HAD TO EXPLAIN TO
SOMEONE WHAT IT MEANS TO

LOVE
until it
HURTS,

WHAT WOULD YOU SAY?

Whoever loves much
performs much,
and can accomplish
much, and what is
done in love
is done well.

VINCENT VAN GOGH

Vincent

On these stars, write things you dream of doing.

Never
end
a single
day
with-
out
being
at
peace with each other.
this is the secret to
preserving love.

POPE FRANCIS

Make peace with someone today.

Reconcile with a friend.

Make that phone call.

 Make the first move.

Before you go to sleep, who do you need to forgive?

THE MOMENTS
WHEN YOU HAVE
TRULY LIVED ARE
THE MOMENTS
WHEN YOU HAVE
DONE THINGS IN
THE SPIRIT OF
LOVE.

Henry Drummond

IN THE HEARTS BELOW, WRITE MOMENTS WHEN SOMETHING YOU DID FOR *someone else* MADE THEIR DAY BETTER.

IN THE
FLUSH OF
LOVE'S
LIGHT, WE
DARE BE
BRAVE. AND
SUDDENLY
WE SEE
THAT LOVE
COSTS ALL
WE ARE, AND
WILL EVER
BE. YET IT IS
ONLY LOVE
WHICH SETS
US FREE.

MAYA ANGELOU

MAKE SOME *resolutions* ABOUT
LOVE FOR THE COMING YEAR.

FILL IN THE BLANKS BELOW:

To love _____ more
would cost me my _____

To love _____ more
would cost me my _____

To love _____ more
would cost me my _____

Someday

... WE SHALL HARNESS
FOR GOD THE ENERGIES
OF LOVE, AND THEN, FOR
A SECOND TIME IN THE
HISTORY OF THE WORLD,
HUMANS WILL HAVE
DISCOVERED *fire*

PIERRE TEILHARD DE CHARDIN

Read over what you've written in this book and write your own definition of
LOVe.

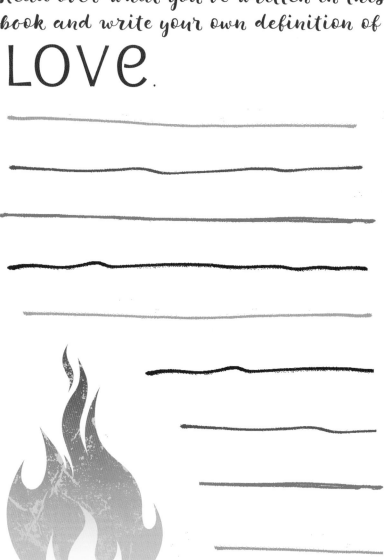